Positive Thinking

Alleviate Tension By Harnessing The Influence Of
Optimistic Thoughts, Contentment, And Affirmations

*(Uncover The Potency Of Positive Thinking And Alter Your
Mindset To Transform Into An Optimist)*

HELMUTH RAMSAUER

TABLE OF CONTNET

Attitude: Reasons Why You Must Use Your Own Thoughts To Overcome Your Problems...1

Reframing's Power: Viewing The World Via A Positive Lens 18

Examples Of Overconscience 40

How Do Beliefs Form?................................57

Advance Your Language Yet.....................72

Seeking Guidance From Role Models And Mentors 106

Attitude: Reasons Why You Must Use Your Own Thoughts To Overcome Your Problems.

Have you ever experienced total paralysis from all of your problems? Even if some of them—like debt or cancer—might be real, pressing problems, what counts in the end is how you see those problems. You can change your mindset more quickly than you can pay off debt or heal a medical ailment.

Focusing on positivity and inner serenity throughout your life can give you the strength to overcome your seeming obstacles. It's not hard to live a life that encourages inner peace.

One time, the author encountered two people at breakfast who had different experiences the previous evening: one had watched the news and had trouble falling asleep, while the other had read the Bible and slept soundly.

Sleep is essential because it restores our vitality, even though it may not appear critical. When you watch the news or have "an earful of difficulty" while trying to sleep, you'll feel restless and unable to work through your problems. Thankfully, you can positively influence this vital energy source.

On the other hand, most people think their situation results from uncontrollable outside events and unfortunate circumstances. However, your world is everything that exists outside of your views about your experiences.

Positive thinking generates factors that lead to advantageous consequences. Conversely, negative thinking leads to unfavorable consequences and can even cause physical illness.

We can see this concept in action by looking at a young man whom the author calls "one of the most complete failures" he has ever met. For a long time, he refused to examine his attitude, which kept him from improving his life. But after realizing that his wretched life was a product of his negative beliefs, he was able to put things right.

Idea No. 5

How to break free from the harmful worrying habit: Don't worry, be happy.

Anxiety and uneasiness are common emotions. Although worrying about your health or finances is understandable, it is detrimental and can affect your personality negatively, in addition to increasing your risk of illness.

Thankfully, worrying is just a bad habit that can be overcome. This specific behavior needs to be broken because it is the root cause of many physical and mental problems. For example, stress brought on by worrying may lead to higher blood pressure, a lower life expectancy, or even arthritis.

But it's rather easy to break the worrying habit—all you have to do is believe you can succeed. If you can imagine it, you can live a worry-free existence. Before you stop a habit, there are several tactics you can use to gain control over it.

All of these tactics include the discipline of clearing your mind or getting rid of thoughts that are bothersome or unpleasant. This is especially important right before bed because our subconscious will likely retain our ideas. Your anxieties, worries, and other negative thoughts could "impede the flow of mental and spiritual force" if you don't get rid of them before they have a chance to become ingrained in your subconscious.

However, clearing your mind alone is insufficient; you must also reload it with positive ideas to replace the negative ones. These are the kinds of concepts that inspire bravery, hope, and faith, among other feelings. You must endure and practice daily to see significant development, even though it could be difficult initially.

advantages of having a positive outlook

There are numerous approaches to boosting your confidence. Some might be more effective for you than others. But remember that to start implementing the changes you want to see, you must truly believe in yourself. Positive thinking increases your chances of success, as demonstrated by healing miracles and perhaps even successful athletes.

Many techniques for boosting self-confidence center on the idea that your body and mind can cooperate to help you achieve desired outcomes. A positive outlook will help you overcome many challenges by enabling you to harness the amazing power of your mind.

Conversely, a pessimistic mindset will lead to negative behaviors, emotions, outcomes, and low self-esteem.

Advice for boosting self-assurance

Make an effort to get rid of negativity from your life.

You may need to reevaluate your closest friends and family if you often doubt yourself. It can be hard, but you must let go of individuals if they are the reason you don't feel confident. Building confidence can be greatly aided by taking a brief break from the individual producing these feelings.

Change the way you carry yourself.

By altering your body language, you can start increasing your self-confidence. Start with your smile, posture, and eye contact. A confident smile with the shoulders back conveys assurance. Smiling will not only make you feel better, but it will also put others at ease in your presence.

Refuse to accept defeat.

Remain persistent and refuse to concede defeat. You possess the ability to resolve any type of issue. How come you would like to give up? One of the most effective ways to increase confidence is to succeed through tenacity and persistence.

Be prepared and ready at all times.

Acquire all the necessary knowledge about whatever challenge you encounter. When you are informed and ready, you will exude confidence.

Section Two

The biggest obstacle to obtaining mental peace is changing your perspective to acceptance and relaxation for God's gift of peace. You must empty your thoughts to receive peace as a gift from God. A tranquil mind facilitates good health and well-being.

You must learn how to purge yourself of any thoughts of regret, remorse, insecurity, hatred, and fear. Relief comes from the simple act of trying to clear your mind. It's crucial to remember that clearing your mind is not sufficient. Something will always enter your thoughts while empty since the mind cannot exist in a vacuum.

A vacant mind is not something that can last forever. Restocking the mind is essential to prevent unpleasant and outdated concepts from resurfacing. You should quickly occupy your mind with constructive and constructive ideas to prevent such a situation. Because the mind will be occupied, the old fears, hate, and worry that have plagued you in the past will not have any room to return.

The easiest way to live is to be peaceful, harmonious, and stress-free. One must learn to live with a different way of thinking. Moreover, words are quite powerful and have certain therapeutic properties. Speaking words of panic will cause your thoughts to get uneasy. On the other hand, a quiet and serene speech will cause a calm mind.

There are useful strategies for cultivating composure and calm attitudes:

Talking with others is one method. We can talk ourselves into feeling anxious, tense, or even angry, depending on what we say and our tone. We can be either good or negative depending on the words we use. For example, if we have a conversation at breakfast that is full of unfulfilled expectations, this will determine the tone and mood for the entire day.

Furthermore, our ideas are directly and significantly impacted by the words we say. Because words are the vehicles for ideas, our thoughts give rise to words. Talking is usually the first step in what we consider to be thinking.

The daily practice of quiet is another strategy for cultivating a calm mind. Everybody must set aside at least fifteen minutes every day for complete silence. Look, find a peaceful spot to sit or lie down and practice the art of silence for fifteen minutes. Steer clear of people, write nothing, and read nothing. Put your thoughts in neutral and try not to think at all.

Let's start simply by saying, "If you want to be happy, be." Don't search for happiness; instead, make it. But to be happy, you must cultivate and uphold a good outlook, make and meet goals, and remember to connect with other people.

Develop an optimistic outlook.

You should understand that your attitude is the source of your happiness. You can't control everything in your life, but you can manage how you respond to it, so work on altering how you think. If necessary, remind yourself aloud that you are responsible for your attitude and behavior. Mentally focus on making the most of the positive aspects of your life rather than trying to correct the negative ones. Essentially, pursue the things that bring you joy.

Furthermore, try not to focus on the bad, particularly how you see yourself. It's a common misconception that working on your shortcomings is less vital than developing your strengths.

Lastly, acknowledge your ability to create happiness for yourself.

Express appreciation

Though it can sound harsh, concentrate on the things you are thankful for. You will experience improved health, fewer depressive symptoms, a more positive self-image, more active connections, and more good emotions by doing this. Develop an attitude of thankfulness by expressing your gratitude, even for small acts of kindness you receive every day. This highlights intimate encounters between people.

Write down the things you are thankful for as well; it instantly helps you feel better.

Take action to lift your spirits.

Your behaviors influence your mood. Try them whenever you sense your mood starting to sour:

-smiling: expressing emotion through movement truly causes the body and mind to experience that sensation.

-Jumping or dancing: this will help even if it may seem foolish.

Remember that you are more than your thoughts.

Get rid of any thoughts that make you feel anxious or depressed right away. Try speaking with a friend or professional if something is upsetting you.

Refrain from passing judgment on oneself.

Give up using the words "should" or "must." These are the words that make you feel more anxious and less motivated to accomplish whatever it is you are thinking of doing. Tell yourself instead that you would prefer to "like" or "hope" to do anything. You will develop a mindset that will encourage you to carry through constructively by doing this.

How to Deal with Nega-Tags

You can ultimately override your Nega tags if you are persistent. A purpose is difficult to remove once it has been firmly established. Until you eliminate it, it remains a permanent part of your mind.

These bad intentions, or Nega-Tags, are deeply ingrained in your mind and manifest as persistent ideas you live with. Your intention statements, which your mind takes to be true, are reflected in what you are currently experiencing in life.

The good news is that once a new intention or consistent idea replaces an old thought, it becomes just as stubborn as the old thought or Nega-Tag it replaced. Existing thoughts and beliefs are indeed difficult to eradicate with new intentions. It would be inconsistent with your new resident's consistent thoughts about returning to where you were.

Our self-talk will reveal our "limits" and Nega-Tags if we notice it. As you can see, intentions have great power because these Nega-Tags function as intents that hold us exactly where we are. Every minute of the day, we use them. They become our recurring thoughts, which mold our lives.

I'll wager that you are probably checking your existing opinions right now to see if you agree or disagree with what you just read. When reading this, have you ever thought, "I agree with you, but I still don't think intention statements will work for me?"? If this is the case, you are confirming that they won't work for you, which is true for you.

For this reason, purpose declarations are among the most dependable tools—possibly even more so than any other. Making sure that the intention you truly want is the true intention is the key to making things work. Our preexisting beliefs will assert themselves and declare, "That's not true," if we say something against what we know to be true. Who are you trying to fool, anyway? We have this Nega-Tag.

When we employ an intention statement, we usually never lose sight of the fact that what we are saying is untrue. It becomes quite simple to undo the intention's entire effect when this occurs.

Setting up your intention statements correctly is crucial to preventing resistance (Nega-Tags) from your subconscious to combat this.

Adding the sentence "It is my intention" to your affirmative statement is the most efficient approach to do this. To demonstrate how this functions, let's go over a few examples.

Declare aloud to yourself:
"I make $100,000 annually."
Say now,
"My goal is to earn $100,000 a year easily and consistently."
Do these claims appear to be different?

Here's an additional one. Tell yourself,

"I have more potential clients or customers than I can manage."

Say now,

"I want to have more prospects than I can manage, whether they be clients or customers."

Do these remarks have a different impact on you?

Which of the claims above seems more plausible to you?

Which of them gives the impression of being contradictory? Which, when you say it, sounds authentic or harmonious?

Which one of these claims prompts the saying, "Who are you kidding? It's most likely the opening statement.

Generally speaking, adding the words "It is my intention" makes something seem more credible and easier to accept and trust. It also removes the Nega-Tag, making its effect much stronger and quicker.

Let's try one more example now to be sure you comprehend the differences completely.

Declare to yourself that you want to:

"I just bought a really nice car."

Substitute something else you do not have for this statement if you own a brand-new luxury vehicle. The aim is to make a statement about something you would like but do not currently have.

Now, note how it feels to say this even though you don't currently own a brand-new luxury car or anything else you claimed to have but don't currently own.

Say to yourself now,

"I plan to drive a brand-new, high-end vehicle."

Which of the two claims do you find most credible? Which of these activates your subconscious'sNega-Tag? Asks, "Who are you attempting to kid?"

You probably have a reservation as you pronounce the first sentence. It appears that some of you are disputing this assertion, thinking things like,

"There's no way I can afford a new luxury car," or "If only that were true!"

However, you'll note that you may make a stronger point when you start the sentence with "I intend," as it makes sense to "intend" to buy a new, high-end car. Since you're not claiming to drive that brand-new, luxurious car, making this claim doesn't require you to utilize your imagination. All you're saying is that you will decide about yourself and work toward that ideal state.

Put differently, adding the phrase "It is my intention" to your intention statement might significantly impact its acceptability. As a result, your subconscious provides you with a positive mental conditioning technique without any opposition. In my experience as a personal performance coach, every client I have worked with has found great success with this approach.

Reframing's Power: Viewing The World Via A Positive Lens

Have you ever been in a scenario where you thought there was no way out, only to find out later that a better option was available? That's what reframing is all about. It goes beyond simply portraying a happy picture. It all comes down to changing your viewpoint to one more empowering.

Reframing is changing our perspective to see a circumstance, someone, or experience in a more favorable light. For example, it can be annoying when a waiter informs you about a backlog in the kitchen. However, you can bond over a complimentary drink if he gives you and your companion a free glass of wine. Should it not have been for the hectic restaurant kitchen, you might have missed that little moment of happiness. As psychologist Barbara Fredrickson points out, this change in viewpoint can transform stress into well-being and widen our brains to new ideas. Reframing can change our emotional response and mentality, from everyday annoyances to important life events.

The Reasons Why Reframing Works, Based on Science

The fundamental tenet of cognitive psychology is that our thoughts influence our moods and actions. Our ideas are negative; therefore, intentionally changing our thoughts can significantly affect our feelings and behavior. Reframing affects how our bodies react to stress as well. According to Harvard Business School research, redefining fear as exhilaration enhanced performance under pressure. In the same way, some people adore roller coasters while others detest them. It all depends on how you see things. When the first drop occurs, will we laugh excitedly or scream? Everything revolves around the picture's frame.

Start by identifying and acknowledging the negative ideas to reframe them. Using mindfulness applications like Headspace or keeping a thought diary can be beneficial. Asking whether these ideas are accurate and whether there is a different viewpoint will help you refute them. Substitute them with a realistically optimistic reframe. For instance, a more realistic way of thinking may be, "I occasionally make mistakes, but I always learn and improve from them," instead of "I always mess up." I learn best from my errors.

The Perfect Reinterpretation: The Lucky Girl Effect

Do you recall the chapter before where I expressed my gratitude for not having a migraine? That's what the Lucky Girl Syndrome is all about. The theory discusses how our minds search for evidence of our deeply held ideas. It's a fresh take on the well-known psychological impact of confirmation bias, which is defined as. Let's just say that I firmly think I'm the luckiest girl alive, that everything is working to support me, and that I am destined for greatness. Imagine, therefore, when one afternoon at the mall, I win a free milkshake. Naturally, I would think, "Of course I won! I'm so fortunate! I see luck at every step when I'm expecting nice things to come my way.

This has a significant effect on reframing as well. All I have to do when I'm irritated is list all the blessings in my life. I'm fortunate to be well, have a reliable automobile, a kind and considerate boyfriend, etc. I could sit here and think about how lucky I am, and it would entirely shift my mood from sour to sweet. I realize it sounds corny, but it improves my mood immediately. The last time we went on a drive, I turned to my brother and said, "Aren't we so happy that we're not running out of gas when we're stuck in a traffic jam?"

Developing a Reframing Habit: Reliability Is Essential

Reframing is a technique that becomes better with use. Reframe one unfavorable idea daily to start small and work your way up. Reframing can be included in your everyday routine, or you can utilize cues, such as a frown or sigh, to remind yourself to do it. Recall that a progressive alteration in thought processes and affective reactions is the aim rather than a sudden shift in perspective.

Looking for the bright side is important rather than ignoring the cloud. It's a reminder that rain is necessary for our growth despite its inconveniences and mess. Reframing may be a potent tool in your positive toolbox with practice, enabling you to face life's challenges head-on and remain resilient.

Section Three

Is There a Monopoly on Opportunity?

Author Frankie questions the widespread perception in this chapter that prospects for success and money are limited and only available to a chosen few. He contends that anyone with the appropriate attitude and strategy may find many possibilities. He contends that one may make their chances for success and wealth by altering how they view opportunities and making progress toward their objectives.

Frankie starts by saying that it is false to think there are only a certain number of chances for success:

"There is no shortage of opportunities for wealth and success. The universe is overflowing with them. The idea that opportunities are scarce and monopolized is a misconception."

He argues that fear and insecurity are the main forces behind scarcity and limited opportunities. He says one might be open to the many opportunities by letting go of these anxieties and beliefs.

Generating Prospects

He outlines the active process of creating chances for prosperity and achievement. He says that one can draw opportunities and seize them by having an optimistic and proactive mindset:

"Opportunities are not something you stumble upon, they are something you create. By having a positive and proactive mindset, you can attract the opportunities you desire."

He encourages readers to focus on adding value for others and discovering their hobbies and talents. He contends that prospects for success and financial gain can be created by adding value and resolving issues.

Getting Rid of Limiting Beliefs

Frankie emphasizes that limiting beliefs must remove prospects for riches and success, limited that thoughts such as "I'm too old" or "I'm not smart enough" can become self-fulfilling and keep a person from recognizing and taking advantage of opportunities:

"Your beliefs about yourself and your abilities have a direct impact on your opportunities. By shifting your beliefs and focusing on your strengths, you can create opportunities that you never thought possible."

He encourages readers to confront constricting ideas and swap them out for empowering ones. He recommends concentrating on one's strengths rather than weaknesses.

Moving Forward

In closing the chapter, Franklin emphasizes the value of moving toward one's goals. He contends that intentional and consistent action cannot be replaced by positive thinking or visualization:

"Opportunities are like seeds that need to be planted and nurtured. By taking consistent and purposeful action towards your goals, you can create opportunities for wealth and success."

He recommends that instead of anticipating quick and noticeable outcomes, one should concentrate on making tiny, gradual progress toward their goals. He highlights that perseverance and focus are disappointments and that success is a process rather than an event.

The Need for Change

Have you ever been caught up in the never-ending web of negativity, where optimism seems like a distant memory and the world is covered in darkness? Have you ever wished for a tiny glimmer of optimism, a hope seed, or anything to keep you going? Yes, I have experienced what it's like to be trapped in the darkness of pessimism, caught up in a maelstrom of intense self-doubt, and pining for even a small ray of hope amidst the pitch-black despair.

Maybe you've experienced the sting of being overwhelmed, the disappointment of having dreams dashed, and the confusing reality of living a life engulfed in negativity. Even worse, perhaps you've just existed as a bystander on life's pavement, where goals are only shattered pieces of unfulfilled ambitions, and joy is a faint echo. It sounds ridiculous, but that's exactly how it is. As those of us who have experienced suffering, you know the depths to which it can go.

The truth is that there is always a route out of the shadows, regardless of where you are coming from or how deep the chasm may appear. A positive-lit route where everyone may enjoy the comfort of knowing they can succeed, make a difference, and get through whatever comes their way! We are taking a whistle-stop trip to learn how to harness the power of positive thought, one of the universe's most powerful forces.

We will take you on a life-changing adventure in the upcoming chapters, one that will lead you from hopelessness to optimism, from negativity to positivity, and from a life of meaningless existence to one full of joy, purpose, and perseverance. We'll explore the incredible potential of positive thinking together, and in just 28 days, you'll see a much happier, more optimistic version of yourself.

If you have me, I will be your mentor and fellow traveler on this fast train of self-awareness and self-transformation. We will rewrite your life's story and show you the way to positivity. But don't be misled—this isn't your typical self-help book. It's an invitation to a life of courageous hope, unfathomable resilience, and endless opportunities.

Acknowledge "The +Point Process."

Our journey is centered around an invention I am passionate about: "The +Point Process." This is more than just a philosophy; it's a method that can change your life and guide you through life's obstacles and your thinking. In addition to rewiring your mental patterns and overcoming life's obstacles with courage, tenacity, and steadfast optimism, The +Point is about accessing the limitless sources of positivity. We will also have a little fun along the way. To put it simply, it's a map—a magnificent, full-color treasure map that leads you from the dangerous territory of negativity to the endless rewards of optimism.

This cutting-edge method will enable you to break free from the constraints that have kept you back for so long, uncover your inner powers, and find the hidden jewels in your potential. It will make you reevaluate your assumptions, widen your perspective, and give your life a fresh lease on life. Our 28-day journey will reveal a new aspect of The +Point Process daily, giving you the knowledge, skills, and attitude you need to create a better, more prosperous future.

Thrilled? Yes, I am!

Welcome on board!

The engine is starting up, the doors covered with graffiti close securely, and the whistle blows. Are you all on board as the train prepares to depart the station?

If so, the radiance of positivity will tear the darkness of despair apart, and your golden Willy Wonka train ticket will transport you there. A place where you will overcome the negativity that permeates our world and find release for your spirit. We will reignite the fires of ambition, drive, determination, and unrestrained success by discovering the keys to changing our lives! Our path is a revolution, not merely one of personal development! - an appeal to defend your entitlement to the efficaciousness of affirmative thought.

Accompany me, and let's illuminate the planet with our radiant positivity!

Five steps to control your pessimistic thinking

It is impractical to expect to get rid of all bad thoughts. Learning techniques to limit your negative thinking will give you more influence over the kind of life you want to lead, making it a more practical and long-lasting strategy.

1. Face your pessimistic ideas. It takes time and experience to master this systematic approach; you won't suddenly be in charge of your thoughts. Prepare yourself and commit to using this tactic every day.

The key to using this method is to educate yourself on how to combat your negative ideas. You have five questions to ask yourself:

Is this idea accurate? Does anything support this unfavorable opinion?

Does this thinking give you power, or does it take it away?

Can you see the bright side of this idea or draw any lessons from it?

Imagine what it would be like to be free of these pessimistic thoughts.

Is this unfavorable idea keeping you from addressing a problem?

2. Put your unpleasant thoughts on hold and concentrate on anything else. Visualization is a helpful tactic to divert your attention from your pessimistic thoughts. Try to visualize yourself engaging in one of your favorite activities: shopping, reading, listening to music, or any combination. The secret is to teach your brain to focus on something entirely different for at least thirty seconds.

Use self-control when attempting this method. Your brain will eventually have been trained to choose an alternative path whenever your pessimistic ideas arise.

3. The balloon workout. Delete your pessimistic ideas. This strategy is my favorite. Essentially, you are

discarding your pessimistic beliefs in this situation.

You can physically discharge negative energy by writing down and letting go of bad thoughts that bother you. Some individuals jot down their pessimistic ideas on paper, which they discard.

I enjoy writing my regrets, anxieties, and pessimism on an inflated balloon and letting it soar into the sky. Discover the method that works best for you.

4. Be in the company of positive people. The individuals you surround yourself with greatly impact your life's course.

Spend time with a friend who exudes positivity and has an optimistic view of life, and if you want to learn how to better control your negative thinking.

5. Change the way you think. Our minds are excellent at tricking us into believing things that aren't true. These false and erroneous beliefs feed into our pessimistic mindset.

The next moment, you quit believing that everything wrong is your fault. By doing this, you are assuming, personalizing, and reinforcing your negative views.

Spend a few minutes praising yourself for all that you have accomplished. Then, write these things down and tell yourself how wonderful you are. One further tactic you could use is refuting these ideas using the questions in serial number 1 above.

In brief."Accepting your thoughts, all of them, even the negative ones. Accept thoughts, but don't become them". This is stated in Matt Haig's book Reasons to Stay Alive.

You may change unhelpful thought patterns with ones that will genuinely assist you in achieving happiness and a sense of peaceful acceptance if you put in the necessary effort and practice. Start thinking positively now.

The Bridge from Imagination to Reality

The solid base of reality is connected to the ethereal world of ideas and dreams through the medium of imagination. It's the power that lets us imagine things that are not possible in the present. Without imagination, dreams would be unfulfilled, and innovation would be suppressed.

Extending the Horizon

The constraints of the here and now do not confine the imagination. The drive pushes us to venture into uncharted intellectual and practical territory and pushes us over our current comfort zones. When we use our imagination, we perceive possibilities where others perceive barriers.

Musk Elon

Few names in history's ever-changing annals evoke the same aspiration, ingenuity, and boldness as Elon Musk. He is a modern-day pioneer, a change agent, and an inspiration source; he is more than just an entrepreneur or a visionary.

Musk's path is proof of the tenacious nature of human endeavor. It is a story about choosing the less-traveled path, facing uncertainty, and changing the direction of one's destiny. Fueled by the conviction that the impossibility is only a challenge waiting to be conquered, he has bravely entered the unexplored fields of space research, renewable energy, and sophisticated transportation, much like a true hero.

Elon Musk is a maverick who has revolutionized industries and rewritten invention rules in a world frequently characterized by caution and compliance. He was a co-founder of Zip2, which was an early example of an online map. Later, he launched PayPal, which completely changed the internet payment landscape. Musk's bold aspirations didn't end there. He established SpaceX, an aircraft manufacturer and space transportation enterprise, to enable human space flight.

But his vision went farther still. Musk transformed the automobile business with Tesla, elevating electric vehicles from a practical to an aspirational vehicle. To harness the sun's power for a more sustainable future, he founded SolarCity as part of his ongoing commitment to sustainable energy.

Elon Musk's story is a live example of the strength of persistence and belief, not just a showcase for business achievement. Musk's pursuits have encountered many roadblocks and doubters, but his unshakable belief in his idea has helped him overcome them, demonstrating that even the most outrageous ambitions may come true.

Imagination and Problem-Solving

In the vast realm of human ingenuity, a profound connection exists between two powerful forces: imagination and problem-solving. They are not mere facets of the human mind but the catalysts for transformative change, the engines that drive progress, and the keys to unlocking the mysteries of the universe.

Imagination is the spark that ignites the fire of human achievement. Every invention, every great work of art, every scientific breakthrough begins with a dream, a vision of something that has never been. It is the audacity to ask, "What if?" and the courage to follow that question into the unknown.

Problem-solving, on the other hand, is the bridge between imagination and reality. It is the practical, hands-on aspect of turning dreams into concrete achievements. It breaks down complex challenges into manageable steps and finds elegant solutions to intricate puzzles.

Problem-solving is the alchemical transformation of ideas into action. It is the determination to overcome obstacles, the persistence to see a vision through, and the resourcefulness to adapt to changing circumstances. It is the grit and the grind, the sweat and the toil that breathe life into the most audacious dreams.

Together, imagination and problem-solving form a dynamic partnership. Imagination provides the vision, the inspiration, and the audacity to dream big. Problem-solving offers the strategy, the resourcefulness, and the diligence to make those dreams a reality. They are like two wings, each necessary for the flight of innovation.

But this dynamic duo is not limited to the pages of history; it is a force that resides within us. We all can imagine and solve. We can dream big and work tirelessly to bring those dreams to life. We can harness the power of creativity to overcome big and small challenges and leave an indelible mark on the world.

Imagination and problem-solving are not exclusive to any particular field or profession. They are the tools of the artist, the scientist, the entrepreneur, and the everyday dreamer. They are the driving force behind innovation, the spark that lights the way forward, and the foundation for the future.

Therefore, let us embrace the creative alchemy of imagination and problem-solving. Let us dare to dream and be relentless in pursuing those dreams. Let us face challenges with unwavering determination, knowing that with each obstacle we overcome, we are one step closer to turning our wildest imaginings into reality.

Examples OfOverconscience

How can you determine whether you think too much? Numerous mental and physical symptoms exist. These could indicate that you overthink things. These are a few of the primary health issues caused by overthinking:

sleeplessness. While not all insomnia is brought on by overthinking, this is a classic sign of it. Do you ever find that your mind starts racing right away when you try to go asleep? Do you find yourself feeling worried, agitated, and unable to fall asleep because you can't seem to control where it goes?

headaches. Numerous factors can induce headaches. They may be brought on by elevated blood pressure or the body's response to physical strain. They may also have psychological origins, such as stress, worry, or depression. One major cause of headaches is overthinking. If headaches are something you experience frequently, overthinking could be the cause.

Joint and muscle soreness. Our bodies are directly impacted by feelings of stress and anxiety. Unknowingly tensing our muscles, we could assume strange positions. Pain in the muscles and joints results from doing this for an extended period of time. Back ache, neck pain, and sore shoulders are possible. Overthinking could be the source of these symptoms if you experience them.

Weary. Our energy is depleted by aches and pains, chronic stress, and lack of sleep. It should come as no surprise that overanalyzingcauses weariness. Overthinking could be the reason behind your persistent fatigue.

Thought patterns can be used to identify overthinking in addition to physical symptoms. The following are a few of the most typical thought patterns connected to overthinking:

Fear and anxiety. Do you have an overwhelming need to organize every last aspect of any upcoming event? Are you worried about what might happen in the future? Do you experience anxiety that seems to have no clear source, or what is known as free-floating anxiety? Have you ever used drugs or alcohol to numb your anxiety? It's normal to feel some worry, particularly when we're looking forward to a tough or demanding occasion. Being anxious all the time is abnormal and could be a sign of overthinking.

Overthinking and failure-related fear. When you consider the future, how does it make you feel? Do you feel at ease and confident? Or do you experience anxiety and feel the need to thoroughly consider every scenario? Do you ever find yourself studying historical events in great detail and becoming obsessed with them? Have you ever put off doing something out of concern that you won't do it well? Being overly analytical is frequently linked to an obsession with controlling your environment. We think we can influence the future to prevent failure by reflecting on the past and potential future events. You can be overthinking if you find yourself going into great detail about everything.

not being in the here and now. There is no turning back what has already transpired. It is impossible to fully control or foresee what may occur in the future. Right now is the one moment in your life that you have complete control over. You cannot fully focus your energy and attention on what you are doing at this moment if your mind is preoccupied with the past or the "What if..." of the future. Doing your best now is the most effective approach to shape the future, with the past being essentially inconsequential. We do less well when we overthink things because it takes our attention away from the here and now.

GAD and overanalyzing

An underlying issue, such as Generalized Anxiety Disorder (GAD), may be connected to overthinking. Anxiety and concern that are persistent and nonspecific are hallmarks of GAD. This indicates that you are anxious all the time rather than being concerned about something specific. and It's possible that you experience panic episodes for no apparent reason at all. You might discover that you are fretting more than is necessary. It's possible that you plan and consider future events all the time.

GAD causes anxieties and fears to take over your life and way of thinking. It prevents you from reaching your objectives and forming wholesome habits. GAD diagnosis might be challenging. It is, after all, quite natural and even beneficial to plan ahead for an upcoming event and think about how to make it a success. Anticipating future events can help us feel less afraid and more confident since we can plan ahead and create plans. There is very little distinction between GAD and healthy thought patterns. You should visit a licensed medical professional for assistance if you think you might have generalized anxiety disorder (GAD).

GAD sufferers experience an unceasing onslaught of intrusive and worrisome thoughts that they are unable to stop or manage. They become mired in a vicious cycle of pessimism, terrified of uncertainty or change. Abrupt, uncontrollably overwhelming feelings of fear and anxiety overtake them for reasons they cannot fathom.

GAD is a prevalent condition. According to the majority of research, GAD affects approximately seven million Americans, or more than 3% of the population, with women being twice as likely as males to be afflicted. Gradually developing, GAD can be brought on by stressful life events and environmental variables. Similar to overthinking, generalized anxiety disorder (GAD) can also induce elevated heart rate, fast breathing, sweating, shaking, and digestive issues.

An sickness of the mind is not GAD. Although some people take medications to lessen the affects of this condition, positive thinking practices can also help those with it.

OCD and overanalyzing

An additional condition that is frequently linked to excessive thinking is obsessive-compulsive disorder (OCD). Similar to GAD, this also frequently shows distinct symptoms of excessive worry. Individuals with obsessive-compulsive disorder (OCD) may believe that they must follow specific rules in order to stay safe. Sometimes they are at least somewhat reasonable, like when someone washes their hands a lot out of a fear of dirt and germs. Sometimes they have no empirical basis as all; examples include an obsession with counting all the blue objects in a room or a need to touch things in a specific order before leaving.

The belief that a specific course of action will result in a specific outcome is the common denominator among all OCD behaviors. For instance, people might think that touching something a specific amount of times before leaving the house guarantees their safety when traveling. Even though they are objectively aware that the two items are unrelated, they are compelled to perform the ritual and experience fear, anxiety, or even panic if they don't.

The degree of OCD severity varies, much like GAD. The majority of people engage in routines and habitual actions that they carry out automatically. Many of us do things like double-checking the front door lock before leaving the house, even if we don't have to. Even though we have closed the door hundreds of times and are aware of when it is secure, we still try it after locking it to be sure. When these habits begin to influence our conduct and how we interact with others, they become a problem. Additionally, they become an issue when we feel anxious and unable to finish these tasks.

Whereas the second way shows you a world where everything is up to you, the first path displays a world where everything is preset. I looked for this road and those doors leading to the pinnacle for a very long time. I spent half of my life wandering, and now that I'm back, I can see the wolves I met and the dark forest I was in. Would I go back in time, or do I regret it? Can pigs fly? It makes no sense to approach life with the idea that you could have handled things differently. The only thing you can say in a situation like this is that it should have been done earlier. Whatever happened, you have to accept it as it was intended to be. It is what it is. I have no regrets because everything that happened in my life has impacted the way I see the world now. I would have a different perspective on everything now if my life had been very colorful. If my queries were different from the book's overall topic, maybe I would look for alternative answers. Furthermore, I wouldn't go down the rabbit hole since it would be preferable to always exist in a delusional state of illusion. I would accept life as it is and go headfirst into any circumstance, good or bad, without realizing that my actions had an affect on it. All you have to do is stay clear of the obstacles that could potentially stand in our way. I now realize that I didn't live a blind life, and it wasn't by accident. Everything that took place was necessary. More than once, I've had enough. And what have I learned from this? I understand what it's like to reach your limit in life. And I'm aware that's not how I want to feel any longer. I now have the confidence to take charge of my life and go in my own direction.

Either directly or indirectly, we are informed that everything has already been discovered, that nothing is beyond our control, and that everything is predetermined. A modern person's primary responsibility is to always strive for a brighter tomorrow while being forced by the system to incur increasing amounts of debt. After looking at many facets of life, I arrived at a particular conclusion. Is it possible that the world's fate has already been decided? This is how I would phrase it: our reality's fate, perhaps not the fate of the entire globe. On the other hand, I know for a fact one thing. It's not real, this planet. This is my next conclusion, which is more grounded in research and real-world experiences than in science. Unless the human misery that exists in this world is what truly makes it authentic. What do I mean by it, though? It has been established by science that the world is theoretically infinite. The idea that the world is made up of atoms is both intriguing and encouraging. Research has shown that atoms are always in motion, even at ever-lower energies. There are an endless number of solutions, based on the behavior and structure of atoms. In reality, empty space makes up almost 100% of an atom's structure. Everything that we see seems genuine—it can be chilly or warm, hard or soft. But as we explore the deeper strata of this physicality, we discover that nothing is fixed in place—everything is always moving. This leads to the astonishing conclusion that everything is actually changeable. Since it seems as a single entity, a solid mass akin to a stone or chair, despite not even being physically attached. What prevents the disintegration of our reality? It feels quite real, and it also doesn't come apart. I'll tell you what keeps you and me and everything you see alive. It's a notion. Things exist because of thought. Building a macro model of our reality from atom simulations would be impossible for us to sustain from a grounded-world standpoint. The first conclusion that quickly comes to mind is this: Life genuinely appears to be a miracle. There's more curiosity in the second conclusion. The idea that ties everything together is not mine or yours; rather, it is the idea of the Creator, or the Programmer. Why does it belong to someone else? Because the world existed before you and I did 20, 30, 40 years ago. The world will most likely still be here when we cease to exist. This is a truly remarkable piece of knowledge, supported more by real-world experiences and research than by strong scientific evidence. In theory, the world should collapse, but it hangs together and doesn't appear to be about to do so. From a human perspective, nothing makes sense other than the idea that some smart person kept everything together. Stated differently, life is what surrounds us and is life itself. This in turn creates more opportunities. Since nothing in life is random and life is life, maybe life is trying to tell us something. Let's investigate the possibility of that.

For centuries, what message has been delivered to us? that the Creator made us in his likeness, correct? If everything was kept completely hidden from us, what enjoyment would there be? Given that this world was, in a sense, the product of someone's imagination, a genius, the creator had a reason for doing so. What comes next, assuming that we were made in the image of the programmer? Are you familiar with this already? Indeed, humans are creative beings as well. Reality is also shaped by our thinking. Like the Creator's thoughts, our thoughts really create reality. The sole distinction is that we were made in the image of our Creator, who is free to do as they wish. It's as though we inhabit someone else's world, or rather, their psyche. We have the ability to affect the world as it appears to us while we are doing it. What is said in the messages? that a holy particle is in each of us. We bear His particle and were made in His likeness. What is meant by that? There is a Divine particle inside every human. What is the population of the world?

Indeed, the number of Divine particles is equal. Is it possible that someone as intelligent as the Programmer wouldn't think of anything like this, that the more Divine particles concentrate on one thing, the greater their power? Do you see what I mean? The greatest actual power in the world to construct reality belongs to mankind. Everybody has the ability to design their own existence. Because we are all made of a Divine atom. Therefore, this power increases with the number of people who jointly develop the same product. Simply put, someone else was aware of this before us and is attempting to take our reality from us by breaking into our hearts. Someone who lacks that power or who, even if they do, need a significant amount of our particles in order to manipulate reality to their will. For the time being, let's go on to something else and disregard the issue of who is poking holes in other individuals. Everyone has the ability to easily make changes in their lives. All you have to do is comprehend the process that makes that possible.

You have two choices in life: to sleep through it or to get up and take action. You have the freedom to choose because, even if it's all prearranged, it is entirely up to you whether or not you participate. I'm thinking about something right now. If the Creator separated His own Being into billions of individuals in some way, perhaps the reason we don't know is a kind of game, in which the Creator Himself presents puzzle pieces and hints to see if we are perceptive enough to interpret the pieces and piece together the entirety of His Being through our consciousness in order to evolve into an even higher form of life. With no primary memory, but with a connection to the Divine and the ability to design our own journey. The Creator must first grasp this, or rather, we must understand this in order to know who we are and where we are going. Are you getting what I'm saying? Our reality is a kind of gaming board, and life is a play and a game. The Creator discovers His own potential via our experiences in life. What He is able to accomplish, what is feasible, and what needs to be avoided. Reason logically; you are both everything and nothing. You are thinking in a huge nothingness. Why amidst an immense nothingness? All you need to do is shut your eyes, or close your eyes before going to bed. Then, what do you see? If it weren't for your physical body, you would be in a huge, empty space. Are you following? He made us in His likeness. As a result, you are in a huge empty space. How do you feel? Most likely nothingness, correct? There must be action taken. Everything began with an idea, and that was the first thing that happened. What concrete things do we currently own in our physical lives? Everything is precisely planned, and everything has a beginning and an end. I wonder if the Creator takes lessons from the events that take place, and if He ever builds a world that is perfect? As things are right now, the game will go on until we accomplish our shared objective, which is the ultimate understanding of the body and spirit being reconciled.

Have you already selected your door, or are you able to view the top of your life? I know which door you've selected if you have as well. I promise that after reading these materials, you will know exactly what is at the top and how to get there, even if you have no idea what's at the summit you're striving for.

How Do Beliefs Form?

Recall that we talked about how your beliefs are what you are genuinely certain of. We need "evidence" to support those views to be certain. We refer to these pieces of evidence as references.

A reference could be as simple as your supervisor complimenting you on finishing a report on time. This acknowledgment lends credence to the notion that "I am competent at my work."

The belief would be stronger the more references you had. For instance, a lovely girl who has been complimented on her appearance since she was little will have thousands and thousands of references attesting to her beauty. She wouldn't need to consider it because her belief would be so strong. She is adamant that she is attractive.

Think of your beliefs as the top of a table, with references as the legs. The table is not able to stand on its own without legs. That is precisely how your beliefs function. Beliefs are formed and maintained via references.

Remove or weaken the legs, and the table top will topple over. Similarly, gathering much evidence against a belief will make it weaker and eventually impossible to hold.

This idea has a lot of strength. It helps us understand how our beliefs function and how to modify them.

To learn more about how references influence our beliefs. It's one of my favorite books about beliefs and NLP.

Now that we have this knowledge, we will apply it to eliminate bad thoughts from our brains and replace them with empowering positive ones.

Strategies that work to alter your beliefs

1. Gather references that support your optimistic viewpoint.

Selectively gathering references for your positive beliefs is one of the most effective strategies to counteract your limiting beliefs while bolstering your positive beliefs.

To do this, consider the two or three most beneficial positive beliefs for you. These are the ideas you think will most benefit you right now. Take a fresh diary and jot down these beliefs on the cover.

Your tabletop, or the beliefs you choose to hold, is this. You need to gather references or facts to support your chosen beliefs.

I want to tell you a very important secret. Your beliefs are stored in your subconscious mind, indifferent to logic or reason. It never questions the rationality of anything.

Give it enough references, and it will accept anything! Any belief you want to have in life is possible for you.

Now, while you go about your day, be alert for anything that might even SUPPORT your chosen views remotely. If one of your chosen beliefs is, "I am becoming a millionaire," for instance, some examples from your day-to-day life to bolster that belief would be: a) I am always on time, much like a millionaire who is punctual. I intend to become one.

b) I put in my best effort at work today, just like millionaires do. I'm capable of becoming a multimillionaire.

c) Like self-made millionaires, I aspire to be a millionaire and am making steps toward that goal. Like them, I am. I intend to become one.

Choosing the belief that "I CAN change myself to become a more positive person" would be a more appropriate example.

Make a conscious effort to see the bright side of things as you go about your day. A reference of belief is even the tiniest instance in which you had a positive thought: "I CAN change myself to become a more positive person."

Noting down these references on paper—or even in the notepad on your phone—is essential in this process. You're compiling a collection of written "references." Never undervalue the impact that written words can have.

Take out your list of day-to-day references and look at it before going to bed. You may now see tangible proof of the good ideas that crossed your head during the day. It significantly increases your self-assurance and fortifies the conviction that "I CAN change myself to become a more positive person."

Your mind needs references and proof that you can change into that kind of person. And nothing could work better than a collection of references from the "real world" you gathered throughout the day.

There could be no end to this list. All it takes is imagination and an optimistic outlook. You might use anything minor and unimportant as a reference. You may even use something terrible as a springboard for your positive, uplifting ideas.

For instance, you work a 9 to 5 job to pay your bills even though you desire to start your own business. You can alter the meaning of the current scenario from "this is such a horrible situation" if you are feeling depressed about it. "I am stranded here," to "What do you know? The cosmos is making me work harder to achieve my objective of starting my own business by putting me through this terrible experience."

Every circumstance may be given a new meaning, and you can use it as a springboard to bolster your self-empowering beliefs. Subconsciously, a lot of individuals do this, but they do it to support NEGATIVE ideas like "people are mean," "money is hard to come by," or "I am not capable."

You'll intentionally do it—for the better ones. Take note of any references you come across (or make) on your phone right away throughout the day to ensure you don't forget them. Write them down in your diary as "evidence for belief" when you go home.

Jotting down your ideas on paper has a magical effect. It gets down to the core of your thoughts. Your accumulated references will give you a strong sense of confidence regarding the belief you have chosen.

You will feel different in four to five days if you keep gathering evidence for your ideas. The conviction will start to seem REAL.

If you keep gathering evidence to support your empowering beliefs—which you should—they will eventually become so embedded in your memory that nothing will ever dislodge them. You'll live a lifetime of firmly-held views.

The Jezebel Spirit Battles Intolerance

It takes forgiveness to be a man or a woman of God. You have to extend forgiveness whenever Jesus Christ asks you to. Many call out to God for relief, but you must forgive those who have wronged you first. I've come to believe that people can be trusted. Sometimes, people seem to be trying to discredit you just to see what you stand for. Anger and hatred stem from an unforgiven past. According to God's word, love is greater than all sins. Wholeness and healing are possible when you apply God's love to your emotions. I now know how to handle problems before they spiral out of control. From God's perspective, your Spirit is extremely valuable. Nothing that is meant to harm you will be successful. As a result, extend forgiveness without delay and avoid letting your incapacity to forgive mar your ministry.

Jezebel's Spirit is jealous.

This Spirit is incredibly obnoxious and prone to jealousy and covetousness. I went through a phase in my life where I lost everything that I considered to be meaningful. I felt that was what I desired as I saw my friends whose lives were not as destroyed. Then the Lord spoke to me, telling me it was time to realize that He was God and to be still. This entails walking alongside him, becoming closer by studying his word, and picking up knowledge from others. I recall just increasing my confidence in God by paying attention to preachers who share insights from the Lord. Even with my meager pay, I knew that all I needed would come to me if I would only wait on the Lord. I didn't only raise my hand. To get the accolades and acclaim I received and where God wanted me to go, I had to put in a lot of effort. I could not let envy get the better of me. Your thoughts are yours to choose. Choose another idea if the first one isn't working.

Despite being told to fast for a year to see the King, Esther remained unenvious of the other ladies. Esther did as she was told, remaining mute. Because of her faithfulness, Esther gained popularity and was distinguished from the other women. She was able to preserve herself and the Jewish people because she followed all of the instructions. Conversely, though.

The Spirit of Jezebel is unaware of Order.

Being too active in several ministries is the ethos behind this. With numerous members, we are one body. Instead of trying to do everything, we should strive to be the best at the tasks God gives us to complete with faithfulness. It is faithfulness that God desires. He tells us to conduct nice deeds because he thinks it would benefit others. To enable God to use his selected ones to advance God's Kingdom, we must constantly be aware of the sequence.

By Nature, the Jezebel Spirit Is in Charge

It even uses others to refine its power and persuade them that their fate is intertwined. Take caution not to get drawn into conflicts that are not yours to wage. Your fate is something you control. Whoever hurt you will pay for it. The people the Lord has called for his purpose are under watchful sight. Never allow somebody to persuade you that you couldn't succeed without them. All signs point to God. He is the only one who is aware of our future's path.

The seductive Jezebel spirit

This is an alluring spirit. Thank God, I have the insight and Spirit to recognize these goliaths and bring them down. The news, social media, television, and advertising all embody the Jezebel Spirit. The Spirit entices men or, in a man's case, destroys women's goals. Yes, males do appear to possess this energy. It can be quite competitive and envious. Never consider it; let discouragement steal their courage. God's word alone can deliver. You don't need to give up since it states, "Greater is he who is in me than he who is in the world." You must maintain your focus on your destiny and not allow the deceptive actions of others to depress you. Women who possess this Spirit think they can be with any man. Whether or not they are married is irrelevant. This is one of the reasons that many of God's workers have difficulty in their walk because of a hindering spirit that prevents the flow of God's Spirit if they are not cautious to wind up. The Spirit is highly spiritual and thrives on pride. This spiritualism can occasionally complicate The leaders' efforts, particularly if they are not constructing on heavenly ideals. Occasionally, the desire to find a new church may indicate a rebellious nature and an inability to accept authority. I've attended many lectures, but I also let myself be disciplined. Going to a different church is something I do not support, especially if God did not direct you there. You will learn to be dependable when you grow where you are planted. In my opinion, you should pray for your leaders and beg God to protect them without intervening. I am quite aware of how people in the church can feel wounded by their leaders. But you have to give God praise for the Bishop of your souls. You ought to kneel daily and offer gratitude for your work, residence, place of worship, town, or area. These geographical locations are all under the holy Spirit's jurisdiction. No one can stop God's holy fire from moving through a community. Jezebel spirits frequently try to enslave people, particularly if they feel called by God to follow a particular path in life. To break free from all of these demonic shackles, you have to start praying. This indicates witchcraft and Satanic bonds need to be broken. Everything follows an order, and you must know how each area's Order works. Always be deliberate and selective in both your speech and cognitive processes. You are the only one who can stop yourself. Your breakthrough is already waiting for you;

you only need to get past your current situation and seize it from the Lord. I have discovered a profound truth about God: the ability to hear his voice. There is such a contrast in his voice. I can relate a personal story of a moment when a stranger seriously harmed me. I approached God for assistance, and just as I was ready to tell him what I needed, the Holy Spirit gave me a very hard squeeze and questioned, "What would God do? Please bless. God was pleading with me so plainly to bless someone, and I thought that person did not deserve the benefit; therefore, my eyes grew wide. The blessing of others is so potent because God will defend you against any weapon that is fashioned against you. Keep in mind that you are unharmed. You are the King's child. Because of the priceless blood of Jesus Christ, you are pure, righteous, and protected. Jesus Christ, and you have the same thinking. God can replenish your strength like eagles when you feel it is being stripped away. Even amid a storm, remember that God controls your life and that His plans for you are good and intended outcomes in line with his holy purpose. God is a provider, and he will. There are no limits to the Jezebel spirit. I used to pray against strongholds, but it is not the same when they are established. You cannot give up on what you have or settle for anything less when you decide you will succeed. Particularly when it comes to your marriage, ministry, and your family members' salvation, you must be steadfast. The Jezebel spirit searches for flaws in partnerships and marriages. The goal is to undermine your faith rather than necessarily breaking these covenants. Never give up on your faith since it is essential to your desired course in life. The idea is that this Spirit will stop at nothing to get what is rightfully yours. It aims to murder, steal, and demolish. Because it is given clear instructions on how to function by sea and serpentine spirits, the Jezebel Spirit takes pleasure in taking advantage of the sexuality of others. These spirits are powerful and well-protected. But the written word has more ability to push this Spirit out of your life, your career, your church, and every other place it appears.

Advance Your Language Yet

Adding the word "yet" to your everyday speech is a terrific way to foster a growth mindset, which gives you the impression that your potential is infinite and that you are capable of great things, according to Stanford psychologist Carol Dweck. Whenever you say something like, "I don't know how to cook yet," or "I can't paint yet," as opposed to, "I don't know how to cook," or "I can't paint," you're implying to yourself that even though you're not now capable of cooking or painting, you might eventually pick up those skills.

Regularly using "yet" in your speech helps you foster possibility and hope, giving you the grit and optimism to face your challenges head-on and discover solutions rather than giving up completely.

The Present

The CEO of Landry's, Inc., which generated $3 billion in sales this year, is TilmanFertitta.Tilman is an American businessman and television personality. He was once approached to advise a young, aspiring business owner. He continued that Everyone has a gift, and the wisest thing you can do is recognize your gift. A gift doesn't have to be singing, dancing, or athletics; it could be something as simple as being exceptionally skilled at conducting interviews or overseeing a project from beginning to end. You must consider your gifts and devise a workable plan to convert those gifts into a revenue stream. If something is missing, teach yourself to state that you are still looking for that something and that you can use your gift as a means of income. Rather than claiming that you don't have somebody to interview, let's say your talent is that you are a fantastic interviewer, but you haven't found anyone yet. Claim that you are still in need of an interview subject or that you are still learning how to operate the equipment. Alternatively, suppose you haven't found your gift yet, and you're still looking for it. Adding yet to your speech will enable you to view your circumstances in a new light. Seeking a solution to your issue will motivate you to take action.

Spend Time With Upbeat Individuals

The well-known proverb "You are the average of the five people you spend the most time with," attributed to self-help author and motivational speaker Jim Rohn, never truly ages. It's true today because the people we spend the most time with shaping our opinions.

It's time to assess your social circle and eliminate harmful influences if you have a pessimistic belief system and find it difficult to solve problems. Take some time to consider how the various individuals you spend the most time with affect your attitudes, feelings, beliefs, and behaviors. Somebody is likely a toxic influence if you feel unappreciated and demotivated after spending time with them.

Reduce your time with them to gradually distance yourself from their influence. Gradually replace their absence by incorporating additional uplifting individuals into your existence. Like negative, positivity spreads easily, and surrounding yourself with positive individuals encourages you to be strong, upbeat, and powerful.

Enjoy a Moment of Gratitude

Research indicates that gratitude enhances life satisfaction, lowers stress levels, builds resilience, and increases self-worth. You feel good and fortunate from the inside out whenever you consider something for which you are thankful, or that gives your life significance, meaning, or happiness. This emotion can give you the strength to overcome obstacles and strive for improvement to bring about your imagined reality.

Develop the habit of thinking about at least one item that brings purpose, worth, ease, and happiness into your life as soon as you wake up. Every two to three hours, briefly express thankfulness by thinking back on one such blessing. You will have shown gratitude for many of your blessings before the end of the day, and you will have created a positive atmosphere for the remainder of the day and the next day.

Positive thinking will become second nature to you, and your troubles won't seem "the end of the world" or catastrophic. Rather, you will view them favorably and use each problem to demonstrate your value. This mindset gives you more power, enabling you to solve issues and improve your way of life.

Let's go on to the next chapter and discover some practical problem-solving techniques to help you fix issues, lessen troubles, and create the life you've always wanted.

Walking With Awareness

Walking mindfully involves taking slow, deliberate strides while maintaining awareness and present-moment awareness. By practicing mindfulness, you should be able to become alert and present in the here and now.

The primary distinction between mindful and ordinary walking is that the former necessitates a full awareness of your surroundings with each step you take and the feel of the earth beneath your feet. By doing this exercise, you'll be able to put your worries aside and take a moment to relax and focus.

In 2013, M. Teut of the Charité-Universitätsmedizin Berlin's Institute for Social Medicine, Epidemiology, and Health Economics published a paper in Evid Based Complement Alternat Med.

The effectiveness of mindful walking as a stress-reduction technique was investigated in this study. Those with high levels of stress were experimented with. The participants were split up into two groups at random by the researchers. While the other group (the waiting group) did not engage in any activity, the first group was required to perform the mindful walking exercise.

The mindful walking group was instructed to complete the activity for forty minutes, with the first ten minutes spent in the present moment. They were instructed to concentrate solely on their sensations for ten minutes. The last 20 minutes had the group being urged to walk regularly. The second group, the waiting group, did not engage in physical activity over four weeks.

The researchers required each group to submit a survey after four weeks to measure their stress. The outcomes demonstrated that although the other group's stress levels remained mostly unchanged from the beginning, the mindful walking group reported less stress and an enhanced quality of life.

Walking with awareness is a form of exercise that you may do anyplace. The stages of walking mindfully are as follows.

Find a place that is calm and serene. This could be a peaceful street, park, or garden. Above all, choose a location that makes you feel comfortable and protected.

Hold motionless and inhale deeply many times. Center yourself and pay attention to your breathing. Breathe deeply and gently, and then release the air slowly.

Focus on each step as you start to move gently and steadily. Observe your leg motions and breaths.

Take in your surroundings' sights, sounds, and scents. Remain fully present in the moment, devoid of any bias or interruptions.

Remain aware of your body. Bring your attention back to your body and the sensation of walking whenever you find your thoughts straying.

Spend at least ten minutes practicing. Make an effort to walk mindfully for ten minutes or more.

Conclude by expressing gratitude. Spend some time expressing your gratitude for the encounter. You have two options: inhale deeply and focus on the here and now, or you can say "thank you" in silence.

You may improve the efficiency of your mindful walking and heighten your enjoyment by using the following advice:

Begin with quick strolls: If you're new to mindful walking, start with short walks for a short amount of time and then gradually expand the duration.

Switch off your phone: To lessen distractions, switch off or silently use your phone.

Walking outdoors: Being outside can help you feel grounded and at ease. If you can, locate a park, forest, or beach.

Pay attention to your breathing: You may maintain your attention and present-moment awareness by focusing on your breathing.

Take note of your physique: Take note of any physical sensations, such as stress or discomfort, and modify your posture accordingly.

Have patience. You must be patient and take your time to notice results. Don't worry if your thoughts stray or the exercise gets too difficult to concentrate on. The more you practice, the more comfortable it will feel.

Practice often. A mindful walking practice should be performed as often as possible or at least once daily.

Use a mantra: Simple mantras like "peace" or "calm" can help you focus and remain in the moment while walking.

Writing in a Journal or Expressive Essay

You can effectively practice mindfulness by keeping a journal and writing expressively.

A paper on expressive writing in anxiety stress coping was published in June 2013 by Andrea N. Niles and five other researchers.

Their study looked at the effects of writing about emotions and how those effects relate to both physical and mental health. Two groups of adults comprised the participants. For roughly twenty minutes, one group was instructed to write down their most upsetting or stressful experiences—or anything completely unrelated—and this task was done four times.

Before and after the writing exercise, the participants' somatic symptoms, anxiety, and depression were assessed. The findings demonstrated the substantial effects of writing on somatic symptoms, anxiety, and depression. It was also noted that writing about one's feelings can benefit those who prefer to communicate their emotions orally or through other means. However, anxiousness is a given for those who repress and don't communicate their feelings.

Journaling can assist with overthinking and mindfulness in the following ways:

It fosters an atmosphere of safety where you may express yourself without worrying about criticism or condemnation.

You can get new perspectives and insights by thoroughly exploring your thoughts and feelings.

It assists you in recognizing and combating negative self-talk and substituting it with realistic thinking and uplifting affirmations.

It helps you deal with and let go of challenging feelings and experiences, which keeps you from dwelling on the past.

It gives you a sense of perspective and distance, which enables you to examine things more objectively.

Encouraging mindfulness, relaxation, and self-compassion lessens emotional distress.

How to Keep a Journal

Now that you know journaling is an effective strategy for overcoming overthinking, let's look closely at the activity.

To help you get started, consider the following steps:

Step 1: Select the Format

Selecting your favorite format is the first thing you should do. There are numerous choices available, such as:

Pen & paper: If you like writing by hand and want to avoid being distracted by technology, this traditional format works best.

Digital: If you prefer to type and wish to store your journal entries on a device or in the cloud, this format is perfect for you.

Audio: If you prefer to express your thoughts out loud or find it difficult to write or type, this format is ideal for you.

Chapter 3: The Principles of Positive Thought

Positive thinking is more than simply a catchphrase or sentimental idea. According to research, positive thinking significantly affects our mental and physical health and well-being. In this chapter, we will look at the science of positive thinking and how it impacts our bodies and minds.

Research has indicated that positive thought practices can enhance and lessen our mood and resilience. Positive thinking increases the brain's dopamine and serotonin, giving us a positive, upbeat feeling.

Furthermore, thinking positively can have a significant effect on our physical well-being. Positive thinking was linked to a lower the American Journal of Cardiology. According to other studies, positive thinking can help lower blood pressure, lessen chronic pain, and potentially lengthen life.

Despite the complexity of the brain, it has been discovered that positive thinking alters its anatomy. Because of a property of our brains known as neuroplasticity, our brains may adjust and change in response to our experiences and actions. According to studies, the prefrontal cortex, the part of the brain linked to happy feelings and making decisions, is more active in those who often engage in positive thinking.

So, how can we apply the discipline of positive thinking to profit from these advantages? Writing in a gratitude diary is one popular method. We may teach our minds to concentrate on the good by making a daily list of the things we must be grateful for. Reframing negative ideas into more positive ones is another tactic. For instance, we could reframe the idea that "I'm not good enough" to something like "I am capable and have valuable skills."

It's critical to remember that adopting a good mindset does not entail ignoring challenging or unpleasant circumstances. Instead, it's about tackling such circumstances with a more growth-oriented and enthusiastic mindset. We may use obstacles as chances for growth and learning if we reframe how we view them.

In summary, ample scientific evidence supports the notion that positive thinking improves both our physical and mental well-being and even modifies the structure of our brains. We can use positive thinking strategies to have happier, healthier lives, such as keeping a gratitude notebook and rephrasing unfavorable thoughts.

IMPACT OF SELF-TALK THAT IS NEGATIVE

Everybody has experienced negative self-talk at some point in their lives. We may have all occasionally engaged in self-talk and negative thinking. This negative self-talk can significantly impact our emotional, mental, and physical well-being. Negative self-talk can seriously hinder our capacity to succeed, enjoy life, and reach our goals. Negative self-talk and how it impacts our lives.

It is crucial to first comprehend what negative self-talk is. The internal dialogue we have with ourselves is known as negative self-talk, and it is frequently judgmental, counterproductive, and negative. It involves ideas like "I can't do this" or "I'm not good enough," which can lead to medical illnesses like headaches, issues like anxiety, sadness, and low self-esteem. Negative self-talk can result in a downward spiral of negative thinking and a low self-image since it effectively teaches our minds to focus on the bad things in life.

A lifetime of programming—frequently impacted by outside forces, including friends, family, teachers, and the media—leads to negative self-talk. For instance, if a youngster hears their parents tell them repeatedly that they are not good enough, they may internalize this message and take it into adulthood as negative self-talk. Similarly, we could form a pessimistic worldview that feeds negative self-talk if we are inundated with unpleasant news.

Negative self-talk can have a variety of effects. For instance, we might never even try to pursue our goals if we truly believe we cannot reach them. On the other hand, we could embark on a project or business, but when things don't work out, we give up because we think it won't work. Additionally, anxiety, tension, and despair brought on by negative self-talk can have a serious negative effect on our mental and physical well-being.

Thankfully, there are strategies for overcoming and countering negative self-talk. Recognizing our negative self-talk tendencies is the first step. We may achieve this by being aware of our inner dialogue and recognizing unfavorable ideas. Upon recognizing our negative self-talk, we can initiate questioning and reframing these ideas. For instance, we can refute the notion that we are unworthy by enumerating our advantages and accomplishments.

Developing mindfulness is another powerful strategy for overcoming negative self-talk. Being mindful entails living in the present moment with all of your attention. We may recognize and eliminate negative self-talk by cultivating mindfulness, which increases our awareness of our thoughts and feelings. For instance, we can utilize mindfulness practices like deep breathing and meditation to help us focus and quiet our brains when feeling nervous.

Another effective strategy for countering negative self-talk is positive self-talk. Speaking to ourselves constructively and encouragingly is known as positive self-talk. To combat our critical self-talk, we can utilize "I am capable of reaching my goals." Positive self-talk can eventually replace negative self-talk with effort and repetition.

To sum up, we are all impacted by the detrimental and ubiquitous phenomenon of negative self-talk at some point in our lives. But we can fight and overcome negative self-talk by being conscious of our negative thought patterns, practicing mindfulness, and using constructive self-talk. Positive affirmations and beliefs can replace negative self-talk, enhancing our general quality of life, emotional and mental health, and sense of self-worth.

"A marvel defeated us," Detroit coach Joseph Schmidt remarked.

Moreover, it was a marvel to others—a reply to a prayer.

Lion linebacker Wayne Walker stated, "God kicked that field goal; Tom Dempsey didn't."

"Interesting. But how is treating Dempsey's story cruel to me?" one may wonder.

Our reply would be, "Very little - except if you foster the propensity for perceiving, relating, acclimatizing, and involving general standards and embracing them as your own. Then, at that point, continue with the wanted activity."

What guidelines could you also follow from Tom Dempsey's narrative, regardless of whether you are truly disabled? Both children and adults can learn and use them:

Significance befalls those who nurture a profound desire to achieve lofty goals.

People who try and keep trying with PMA achieve and maintain their success.

It takes practice to become an expert in any human movement.

Continue practicing.

Work and exertion can become enjoyable if you establish clear goals.

Every setback provides a beginning of equal or more advantage for individuals motivated by PMA to become achievers.

Man's strongest suit is his ability to petition for things.

Turn your undetected charm to the PMA side to understand and implement these requirements.

Henley may have been telling us that we are in charge of our destiny since we were the foremost authorities on our viewpoints when he wrote the lovely lines, "I'm the expert of my fate, I am the commander of my spirit." Our mindset determines our future. This rule applies to everyone. Whether or not the mentalities are beneficial, the artist may have conveyed to us, with remarkable emphasis, that this regulation is effective. The law states that we must translate our beliefs and concerns into reality. We translate thoughts of neediness into reality as quickly as possible.

Thoughts of plenty. However, we attract vast and generous swaths of advancement when we behave outstandingly towards ourselves and are liberal and tolerant towards others.

A truly amazing individual. Consider Henry J. Kaiser, who has been incredibly successful due to his amazing self-discipline. Over a billion dollars worth of resources are available to organizations named Henry J. Kaiser. His generosity and compassion for others have allowed the bewildered to speak, the wounded to recover from a precious life, and innumerable others to receive emergency medical care at incredibly little cost. His mother had sown ideas in him that eventually led to this.

Henry was the recipient of the incredibly precious gift from Mary Kaiser. She also taught him how to live life to the fullest every day.

1. The Priceless Gift: Following her typical workday, Mary Kaiser would spend hours volunteering her medical skills to help the unfortunate. She frequently said to her kid, "Henry, nothing is at any point achieved without work. On the off chance that I leave you only the will to work, I have left you the invaluable gift: the delight of work."

2. The Most Important Thing in Life: "It was my mom," stated Mr. Kaiser, "who previously showed me probably the best qualities in life. These incorporated the adoration for individuals and the significance of serving others Loving and serving individuals, she used to say, is the best worth throughout everyday life."

Henry J. Kaiser is aware of PMA's power. He knows how it might affect his life and his nation. He is also aware of the power of NMA. He amazed everyone by assembling more than 1,500 boats so quickly during World War II. The experts responded, "It can't-it's unthinkable!" whenever Keizer declared, "We can fabricate a Liberty Ship at regular intervals," but Keizer succeeded. Those who concede they cannot suppress their positive traits turn to their flaws. Those who embrace their ability to combat pessimism use the bright side.

Therefore, we need to use caution when using this charm. All of life's abundant blessings can be offered to you by the PMA side. It can help you overcome obstacles and identify your strengths. It can support you.

Just as with Kaiser, you can make what people believe is unthinkable happen when you walk in front of your opponents.

However, the NMA side is just as powerful. It can bring about pain and defeat instead of accomplishment and satisfaction. The charm is dangerous if we don't use it properly, just like any other power.

How repellent NMA's force is. A very captivating narrative illustrates how the NMA's force repels. It originates in a state in the South. There, where wood ovens are still used to heat homes, continued equally futilely. Woodworker. He had provided kindling to a certain mortgage holder for over two years. The woodcutter calculated that if the logs fit this chimney, their width could not exceed seven creeps.

This elderly customer once asked for a wooden string, but when it was delivered, it was gone. When he returned, he discovered a larger portion of the wood than the designated area had been taken. He asked the woodcutter to split or swap the larger-than-usual logs when he gave him a call.

The wood seller exclaimed, "I can't do that!" He hung up after saying, "It would cost more than the entire burden is worth."

Thus, splitting the logs himself fell on the mortgage holder. He set off to work, concentrating. Halfway through the gig, he discovered that someone had blocked up an incredibly large button opening on one log. The owner of the property raised the log. It had all the signs of being vacant and seemed oddly light. Using a forceful blow to the hatchet, he broke the tree trunk.

A roll of aluminum foil dropped out and discolored. With a bow, the mortgage holder took out the roll and unfolded it. It was astonishingly old, with $50 and $100 bills. He counted them one by one. They came to exactly.

$2,250. Because the paper was so weak, it was clear that the notes had been in the tree for a very long time. The owner of the property had PMA. His principal plan was to give the money back to its rightful owner. After getting the phone, he called the lumber dealer and inquired where the heap had been cut. The logger's NMA once more shows its heinous might.

"That is no one's business except mine," he replied. "If you reveal your secrets, people will inevitably work against you." The mortgage holder made multiple attempts but could never find out who fixed the cash in the logs or where it originated.

This story's place is not in its incongruity. The evidence clearly shows that whereas the man with NMA did not see the cash, the man with PMA did. But it's also a fact that everyone experiences amazing breaks in life. Nevertheless, the person with NMA will prevent the good things in life from coming to him. The PMA sufferer will also control his mood to turn even the terrible setbacks into advantages.

Al Allen, a sales representative, was a key player in the Combined Insurance Company of America's commercial power. Al tried to implement the PMA criteria from the helpful books and journals he read, determined to become the organization's top sales representative. Soon after reading "Foster Inspiring Discontent," an article in Success Unlimited magazine, he got to put what he had read into practice. He suffered a terrible blow. This allowed him to control his stance and effectively use his PMA side of the charm.

He produced shifting dissatisfaction. Al "cold analysed" every business on a Wisconsin city block one freezing winter's day; he just wandered in and tried to sell insurance. That day, Al didn't close any sales. It was obvious that he was unhappy. Al's PMA, meanwhile, turned this letdown into "motivating disappointment."

Using Failures as Learning Opportunities

Setbacks are an inherent part of life. Everybody encounters difficulties and misfortunes that might leave us feeling hopeless, disheartened, and inclined to quit. But it's precisely at these trying moments that our resilience and true strength are tested. These are the times when we can let our failures define us or turn them into opportunities to grow and achieve more.

The book Fueling the Fire Within Discovering Motivation for Success aims to uplift and encourage those facing difficult circumstances. It's a manual that will assist you in turning obstacles into chances for improvement and self-improvement. Through effective motivation, you may conquer any challenge and come out on top.

The idea that obstacles are only momentary detours on the way to achievement rather than permanent obstructions is one of the primary concepts this book explores. You can use these failures as stepping stones to reach your goals by changing how you think about them and adopting a positive viewpoint. It's important to remember that failure is only a roadblock on the path to achievement rather than the destination.

Fueling the Fire Within offers effective techniques and doable measures to assist you in getting through difficult times through true accounts of people who have overcome great obstacles and won over adversity. It provides advice on how to keep up your motivation, preserve a growth mindset, and cultivate a resilient outlook that will help you get through any obstacle.

This book also explores the value of having a strong support system around you and the strength of self-belief. It highlights the importance of persistence, resolve, and an optimistic outlook as necessary components of success in life.

Fueling the Fire Within can remind you of your innate strength and potential while reigniting your motivation in the face of personal or professional failures. It will act as a ray of hope and motivation, inspiring you to keep going despite the difficulty of the road.

In conclusion, changing one's perspective to see failures as learning opportunities requires tenacity and resolve. You may turn adversity into opportunity using the techniques and skills found in Fueling the Fire Within Discovering Motivation for Success. By adhering to these principles, you may overcome difficult circumstances and become stronger, more driven, and ready to succeed in all facets of your life.

Chapter 4: Leveraging Your Environment for Inspiration

Having Positive Influences Around You

It's critical to surround oneself with supportive people throughout difficult times so they can ignite your inner fire and provide you with the drive to succeed. People, places, and behaviors are just a few of the sources from which these impacts might originate. You can overcome challenges and find the willpower to never give up by making the deliberate decision to surround yourself with positivity.

The people you spend time with and surround yourself with greatly impact your life. The proverb that reads, "You are the average of the five people you spend the most time with," is applicable here. Having people around you who are positive, tenacious, and growth-oriented can greatly affect your drive to succeed. Find friends, mentors, or coworkers who have accomplished the goals you have for yourself. Their experiences, advice, and encouragement can be a potent source of inspiration, reassuring you that achievement is still achievable despite difficulty.

Furthermore, it's critical to establish a setting that inspires motivation and optimism. Decluttering and arranging your physical area to encourage creativity and productivity might be easy. Adorn your surroundings with inspirational sayings, self-affirmations, or pictures representing your ambitions and aims. Having inspiring images all around you can help you stay motivated when things become hard by constantly reminding you of your goals.

Developing positive habits can also significantly impact your motivation for achievement in general. Establish a morning regimen of exercises, reading uplifting books, or meditation to start your day. These routines can help you establish the mood for the day and give you the mental and emotional strength to overcome obstacles head-on. Maintaining consistent positive behaviors will help you become more resilient and motivated, allowing you to overcome obstacles without losing sight of your objectives.

In conclusion, it's critical to surround yourself with supportive people throughout trying times so they can stoke your inner fire and provide you with the drive you need to succeed. Surrounding yourself with the proper people, establishing an environment that encourages happiness, and cultivating good behaviors are all critical components of this process. Remember, success is not guaranteed to be easy, but by embracing positivity and motivation. Never quit; keep fanning the fire within.

Seeking Guidance From Role Models And Mentors

Feeling overwhelmed and discouraged is a normal reaction to hardship and obstacles. It can be challenging to carry the burden of our difficulties by ourselves, and the road to success might appear difficult. But it's at these difficult times when looking for guidance and inspiration from mentors and role models becomes essential to stoking the inner fire and finding the will to never give up.

Mentors and role models can raise, motivate, and guide us when we most need it. They have the knowledge and expertise to guide us through life's choppy waters and help us become stronger and more resilient. We can obtain insightful knowledge and perspectives that can change our perspective and help us succeed by drawing on their experiences and learning from their successes and disappointments.

Knowing that we are not alone in our challenges is one of the biggest advantages of asking mentors and role models for help. Their experiences and struggles are similar to our own, and their tales remind us that we can all overcome what we set out to do. We are inspired to endure by their tenacity and determination, which serves as a reminder of our potential.

Furthermore, mentors and role models can offer us helpful guidance and successful tactics. They can assist us in determining our assets and liabilities, establishing realistic objectives, and creating strategies to go beyond roadblocks. Their advice and assistance can help us hone our abilities, make wise choices, and maintain focus as we work toward achievement.

In addition, when we most need it, mentors and role models can provide emotional support and encouragement. They can lend a sympathetic ear, impart insight, and relate their tales of overcoming hardship. Their faith in us can give us fresh assurance and self-belief, empowering us to take on even the most difficult circumstances head-on.

In conclusion, getting help from mentors and role models is a crucial first step toward finding success motivation, particularly in trying circumstances. Their insight, direction, and support can enable us to rise above hardship, cultivate perseverance, and never give up on our goals. We can discover the inspiration and drive to fan the flame within and accomplish greatness in our lives by accepting the teachings and experiences of those who have gone before us.

Accomplished.

Researchers have also found an intriguing link between health and optimistic thinking.

Regardless of a patient's faith, praying for them expedites their healing. The benefits of prayer on patients are evidence that it is effective; it is simply positive thinking.

Laughter is a healthy feeling and action that promotes healing. Laughter has the power to relieve stress, pain, and blood pressure. It's true what they say—"laughter is the best medicine."

Chapter 2: Biases and Negativity Effect

When a situation might be either positive or unpleasant, humans tend to focus on its negative aspects.

In essence, the principle of survival of the fittest has enabled us to transition from apes to humans. As a result of this evolutionary process, we have acquired some remarkable skills.

Making assumptions based on stereotypes is one of these skills, and both emphasize negative traits more than positive ones.

Before we get too carried away, stereotypes are useful tools that have helped us in the past.

Everything is neatly packaged into small containers we may keep and retrieve as needed. Since humans are habitual beings, arranging habitually has aided us in overcoming obstacles from monkey to human.

The organization helps us remember and remembering helps us with almost everything. Our brains are wired for order.

When we make assumptions, such as assuming anything based only on its appearance, the issue with stereotyping becomes clear.

However, evolution has determined that presumption and stereotyping are essential to survival; hence, it has always been "safe" to focus on the possible negative. This challenges modern people when they encounter a person, location, or object they are unfamiliar with.

We tend to compare something we have experience with, even if we have no firsthand knowledge of the person, place, or item in question. Hence, we make assumptions and stereotypes.

Stereotyping and assumptions are seen as bad habits to get into since they hurt our sensitive modern sensibilities.

Even though stereotypes and assumptions are frowned upon in today's society, our subconscious tolerates them.

Although it is socially inappropriate to generalize and harmful to assume, people stereotype daily, and the subconscious responds.

In actuality, negativity bias, often known as the negativity effect, is a new moniker applied to stereotyping.

The Negativity Effect/Bias is experienced by people when they conclude people, places, or things based only on unfavorable stereotypes or when they make negative judgments about them.

Examples of Negativity Bias or the Negativity Effect in Individuals, People, or Groups: "My former spouse betrayed me and told lies about it." Men are liars and cheaters.

Location/Situation: "My friend stayed in a hotel during her Hawaii vacation, and now her home is infested with bedbugs!" Hawaii is a filthy destination with many bedbugs, and I wouldn't want to travel there because of the bedbug infestation in hotels.

Items/Things: "John was using the copy room printer, and there was a paper jam." Paper always gets jammed in printers, making them ineffective.

These are little instances, but they demonstrate how the negative bias and the negative effect permeate our minds.

We would not have enough time to comprehend all the information if we tried to individualize every person, place, and thing we encounter throughout our lifetimes.

Are we destined to rely only on unfavorable preconceptions and stereotypes? No, without a doubt. We may overcome negativity by adopting constructive attitudes and actions.

Easy Reminders

When offered an option, the brain leans toward the negative

Give the brain no options. emphasize the good above the negative

Consider and defend any unfavorable preconceptions or assumptions you may have.

Things don't always go your way, and bad things happen, but you give them power over your life, and that is all.

While admitting mistakes is OK, characterizing them as failures is not. Rather than pulling you down and submerging you in failure, mistakes have the power to inspire you to reach new heights of success.

Easy Reminders

Put an end to negative ideas as soon as they emerge. Give up!

Justify your pessimistic ideas, speak to yourself, and ask why.

Put your bad ideas and emotions in writing in a notebook.

Engage in an activity you enjoy and replace negative thoughts with constructive actions.

Your subconscious will be more open to positive connections and presumptions the more actively you try to shift from negative to good.

Your perspective of people, places, and things will shift if you challenge negative thoughts as soon as they arise and put an end to them because negativity is a subjective state. Keep your self-perceptions honest and avoid inflating any negative aspects of yourself.

Never shirk accountability for your deeds; self-reflection is the only way to make positive thinking work.

If you don't accept responsibility for your actions, noticing negative thoughts and replacing them with positive ones might be challenging.

Consider your actions carefully; if you are at fault, own up to it and move on. Own it and let it go—denial simply fuels more negative ideas and behaviors.

www.ingramcontent.com/pod-product-compliance
Lightning Source LLC
Chambersburg PA
CBHW052157110526
44591CB00012B/1979